Discover American Ind

The Family's Journey	2-3
The Suquamish	4-5
Travel Activities	6-7
The Hopi	8
Travel Activity	9
The Lakota	10
Travel Activities	11-15
The Ojibwa	16-17
Travel Activities	18-19
The Onondaga	20-22
Travel Activity	23
The Cherokee	24-25
Grandma's House	26-27
Pronunciations/Books	28
Answers	inside back cover

G000042011

PHOTOS

"Andrew," called Mr. Young. "Did you pack your outfit for the powwow?"

"I sure did, Dad. But I forgot my Walkman," Andrew answered as he ran back into the house.

Sarah chimed in, "I've got my photographs of Scout camp to show Grandma. Do you think she has pictures of herself when she was little?"

Mrs. Young nodded as she closed the front door after Andrew. Mr. Young slammed the trunk closed, and the family excitedly took their places in their new convertible.

They were finally on their way!

The Family's Journey

Sarah and Andrew already know a lot about their American Indian heritage. They know their Cherokee creation story that tells how their tribal nation began, and they also know that most scientists believe that Christopher Columbus was not the first to discover the New World. These scholars believe that thousands of years earlier, people found a way to migrate, or move, into the New World. Gradually these people spread from the northwest part of the continent throughout North America. Eventually they settled in different areas, becoming many groups of people, including the **Cherokee, Hopi, Lakota, Ojibwa, Onondaga,** and **Suquamish** tribes. When Amerigo Vespucci, another explorer, met some of these people, he mistakenly called them "Indians," because he thought he had landed in the country of India.

The various American Indian tribes developed different ways of living, depending on the land, weather, plants, and animals where they settled. Those who lived in the Northwest, for example, had plenty of trees to build houses and lots of fish to eat. The Native Americans in the Southwest had to find a way to grow crops in a dry, hot climate. The groups in the Plains, the Great Lakes, the Northeast, and the Southeast each faced other conditions and natural resources.

The Youngs plan to visit a tribal nation in each of these six regions to see how these groups live now and to learn a little about their past. You can discover where these nations are located by (1) unscrambling their names and (2) writing their names by their number on the map. (Psst. You'll find their names in heavy type above.)

Now find out how many miles the Youngs will travel. First, place a piece of paper right under the Mileage Key chart and copy the mileage lines on the edge of the paper. Then write the miles under the lines. Use your chart to measure the Youngs' routes between each tribe, and write the miles on the Mileage Chart. Begin at no. 1 and measure the length of the arrows to no. 2. How many times does your chart fit along the arrows? After you measure the five routes and add the five numbers, you will discover how many miles the family will travel.

1. qususmiha _____
2. ohpi _____
3. aaktol _____
4. oajbwi _____
5. nooangda _____
6. ehceorke _____

> **?** **WHO ARE THE LAKOTA?**
> You probably know this tribe as the Sioux, but they prefer to be called the Lakota.

Massachusetts

NORTHEAST
TRIBES

Rhode Island

New York

4.

Wisconsin

5.

South Dakota

Pennsylvania

Iowa

3.

Nebraska

GREAT LAKES TRIBES

Indiana

GREAT PLAINS TRIBES

North Carolina

6.

Oklahoma

Tennessee

South Carolina

Texas

SOUTHEAST TRIBES

Mississippi   Alabama   Georgia

Florida

MILEAGE CHART

Between 1 and 2: _____ miles

Between 2 and 3: _____ miles

Between 3 and 4: _____ miles

Between 4 and 5: _____ miles

Between 5 and 6: _____ miles

_____ total miles of trip

MILEAGE KEY

0   300

100   200

Hurrah!

The A-mazing Suquamish Cycle

Mrs. Young volunteers at the Suquamish Museum, and the family stopped there to drop off a package. The Suquamish tribe is one of many Puget Sound Salish tribes. Today, many tribal members live throughout the United States. However, their homeland is the Port Madison Indian Reservation near Seattle.

Back in the 1800s, people of this Northwest Coast tribe lived very differently than they do today. Between November and March they lived in villages consisting of plank houses. These were long wooden houses used by several families. During the spring the Suquamish moved to temporary camps near rivers and forests. In the rivers they built wooden fences, called weirs, to trap salmon, their main food. As the fish collected at a weir, men could spear them easily. In the forests the men hunted deer, elk, beaver, and other animals, while the women and children gathered berries, plants, and shellfish. They preserved the extra food for use during the winter.

Here is a maze. It is March and the Suquamish are leaving their winter village for their forest camp. Help them find their fishing weir *and* a place among the tall cedars to build their summer houses. Along the paths you will find numbered letters. Write the letters on the numbered lines below to find out why the Suquamish moved in the spring and the fall.

6, V

2, O

3, S

5, R

8, V

9, E

4, U

7, I

1, T

___ ___   ___ ___ ___ ___ ___ ___ ___
1   2   3   4   5   6   7   8   9

Tree-mendous Woodworks

As the family drove through the forests of tall red cedar trees in Washington State, Mr. Young told the children that in earlier days cedar trees were vital to the Suquamish people.

Mrs. Young added, "They're *still* important!"

"You're right," Mr. Young continued. "But in the past, like all American Indians in the Northwest, the Suquamish made many everyday things from the wood, bark, and roots of cedars. They collected cedar bark in the spring by pulling long strips from the trees. After they removed the outer layer, they beat the inner bark to soften it, so they could work with it."

Below are four objects that the Suquamish made from cedar trees. Guess how these items were used. If you need help, look at the modern objects at the bottom of the page.

A _____

B _____

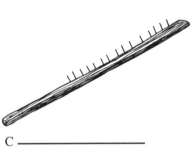

C _____

D _____

Now unscramble the words below and find out what part of the cedar tree the objects above were made from. You will also discover other things the Suquamish made from this wonderful gift of nature.

Made from Wood

acneo _____

ddpale _____

owlb _____

oospn _____

rttael _____

lswhiet _____

ooml _____

lucb _____

kera (to catch fish)

_____

oolts _____

uoseh _____

Made from Inner Bark

ath _____

peac _____

tsrik _____

pedair _____

rstngi _____

tskeba _____

atm _____

lpilwo _____

lodl _____

Made from Roots

skbtae _____

You will find the following objects:

basket (twice)
bowl
canoe   paddle
cape   pillow
club   rake
doll   rattle
diaper   skirt
hat   spoon
house   string
loom   tools
mat   whistle

Many Tribal Nations

"Hurray, we've finally left Washington," Sarah cried.

"Yeah, Hopi nation, here we come!" chimed in Andrew as he waved his arms.

"Do you know how many American Indian nations there are?" Mr. Young asked.

"Not really," Andrew answered. "About one hundred?"

"More than that," Mr. Young smiled. "There are around five hundred tribes in the United States today. And you can find American Indians in each of the fifty states."

"Did all the tribes from the Northwest live like the Suquamish?" Sarah asked.

"Good question," Mr. Young said. "Because they lived in the same type of environment, they had and still do have similar ways. But every single tribe has its own culture, lifestyle, customs, and language."

"I can't wait to see how the Hopi Indians are different from us," Sarah exclaimed.

"You will notice differences," Mrs. Young commented. "But I bet the kids there listen to the same music you do." With that, Mrs. Young gave the children a tribal nation word search to help pass the time.

You can do it too. You'll find ten tribal nations: **Calusa, Chickasaw, Comanche, Iowa, Miami, Miwok, Narragansett, Navajo, Susquehannock,** and **Yakima.** All ten nations go *across* the word search. For each nation, one of the states where its members live goes *down* and *overlaps the nation.* You will find the following ten states: **Arizona, California, Florida, Indiana, Iowa, Mississippi, Pennsylvania, Rhode Island, Texas,** and **Washington.** The first one is done for you.

Now find these ten states on the map on pages 2-3 and write the correct tribal nations in them. (Of course, other tribes live in each of these states too.)

Yuccas and Mesas

Sarah looked up from her reading and exclaimed, "Wow, look how different everything looks here!"

"Yeah," Andrew responded. "I don't see any trees, and look how flat that mountaintop is!"

Mrs. Young answered, "That's a mesa, Andrew. We're now in the Southwest, where the deserts are very hot and dry. Not too many plants can grow here, and they're very different from the ones we grow at home. See the one that looks like a tall white candle? It's a yucca."

"Is that a dog over there?" asked Andrew.

"No," Mr. Young replied, "I think it was a coyote. Coyote, by the way, is a joker in many American Indian stories."

"I just saw a sign for the Navajo Nation," observed Sarah. "What's that?"

"That's the name of the reservation where the Navajo live. Some people now call them Diné," Mrs. Young responded. "Some Navajo still live in hogans. See if you can spot any of these houses—their roofs are rounded."

"The Navajo are well known for their weaving," Mr. Young added.

"I bet they use the wool from those sheep over there." Sarah was proud of her observational skills.

"They also grow a lot of corn," Mr. Young continued. "Corn is really important to all the tribes in the Southwest."

The whole family was eager to explore this exciting new environment. You can, too, by circling nine things that do *not* belong in this picture of the Navajo Nation. Why don't they belong here?

A **reservation** is a tract of land set aside by the U.S. government for American Indians to live on. Use an encyclopedia to find out more.

His and Her Gifts

The Youngs arrived in the Hopi village of Moenkopi in time to help celebrate the wedding of Lynn Talayesva, Mrs. Young's college roommate. Mrs. Young told Andrew and Sarah that many Hopi couples are married in a civil or church ceremony first, and then have a traditional Hopi wedding months or even years later.

"As you will see," said Mrs. Young, "the families of the bride and groom spend a lot of time making special gifts for each other. These gifts help to build strong bonds between the bride and groom and their families."

Andrew and Sarah learned that each family has special jobs. Before the ceremony, the bride goes to the home of the groom's mother and spends three days grinding corn into meal and baking *piki,* a special type of cornbread. "Because corn is so important to Hopi existence," said Mrs. Young, "it is also important in the wedding preparations. Both the bride and the corn are seen as givers of life."

Mrs. Young then explained how the male relatives of the groom spend many hours spinning cotton and

weaving two special wedding robes for the bride. During the wedding she wears one of these robes and carries the other in a special reed case. She will be buried in the one she carries when she dies.

"On the fourth day of the wedding, after a brief prayer service," Mrs. Young continued, "the bride and a crowd of friends and relatives parade back to her mother's home. Everyone brings gifts and food for the feast. At a later time the bride's family contributes great quantities of cornmeal and many trays of *piki* in a payback procession to the groom's family home."

"Wow," exclaimed Sarah. "I can't wait to join the celebrations!"

Hopi women grind corn into meal to make *piki* using a special set of grinding stones. See if you can turn CORN into PIKI by changing one letter at a time. Use the clues to make a word.

CORN

— — — —   (middle of an apple)

— — — —   (not less)

— — — —   (skin opening)

— — — —   (to prod or jab)

— — — —   (type of fish or superhighway)

PIKI   (paper-thin cornbread)

Weaving is traditionally a Hopi man's activity. See if you can make this man's ROBE into a GIFT for his bride.

ROBE

— — — —   (a flower)

— — — —   (opposite of win)

— — — —   (missing)

— — — —   (storage area in barn)

— — — —   (to raise)

GIFT   (what groom gives bride)

A Sense of Place

"I love the sound of Hopi names," Andrew said as they headed north again. "I think I'll keep a list of every Indian name I see for the rest of the trip."

"Good luck!" smiled Mr. Young. "That will keep you *very* busy. Many Americans speak an American Indian language every day and don't even know it! For starters, over half the states in the U.S. have Indian names. Just look at a map and you'll see many cities, towns, mountains, and rivers with names that came from Indian beginnings. Many places were named for features of the land, but others are connected with tribes, individuals, or events that happened nearby. For example, *Moenkopi* is Hopi for "place of running water," *Iowa* is a Great Plains tribal name, and you know that *Seattle* is named after Sealth, the Salish chief."

Tracing the history of Indian names can be confusing. Some names were spelled by early traders and explorers who didn't know the language. The Europeans wrote what they heard in whatever language the Native Americans spoke. Just imagine how a name changed as it passed from American Indian to French trapper to English soldier to German missionary! However these Indian place names are recorded, they are a window to American Indian history and a reminder of the deep relationship between Indians and the environment.

Below are six places in the Northeast that have Indian names. You can find out what these names mean by working this puzzle.

* First, look at the Indian phrases and their meanings below. Then use these meanings to figure out what the parts of each place name mean. (Remember, spellings often change over time.)
* Next find a feature on the map that matches the meaning.
* Finally, write the letter of the map feature in the circle in front of each place name.

Indian Phrases	Their Meanings
hanna	stream
atin	hill
manah	island
kit	great
loyal	middle
sisku	muddy
tunk	small

◯ *Loyalhanna* means _____ _____

◯ *Kittatinny* means _____ _____

◯ *Manhattan* means _____ _____

◯ *Kittanning* means _____ _____

◯ *Tunkhannock* means _____ _____

◯ *Susquehanna* means _____ _____

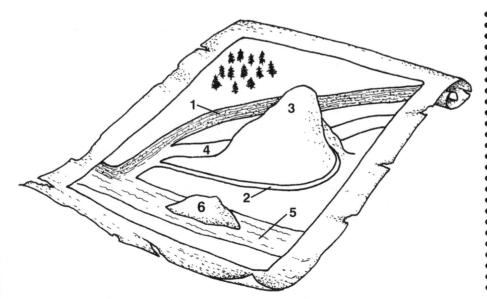

Of course, not all American Indian names came from the same language. Just imagine! More than 2,000 different Indian languages were spoken in North, Central, and South America.

Aunt Lucy's Graduation

As the family neared Pine Ridge, the Lakota reservation where Uncle Gordon and Aunt Lucy live, Andrew exclaimed, "Boy, you can see for miles in South Dakota! And there's grass everywhere!"

"Yes, and where are all the trees we have in Washington?" Sarah asked.

"All of this region looks like this, and so the Lakota and other Great Plains tribes used to live very differently from the Suquamish or the Hopi," Mr. Young responded. "We'll tell you more about the Lakota later. Right now we must hurry so we won't be late for Aunt Lucy's graduation."

"I can't wait to see her graduate," Sarah cried.

"Yes, it was difficult for her to work and go to college at the same time. But Oglala Lakota College is right on the reservation and helps young Native Americans get a good education."

"Look, there's the entrance to the Three Mile Creek Powwow Grounds," Mrs. Young interrupted. "We're to meet your aunt and uncle there."

After lots of hugs the family found seats, and the children looked at their programs. On the cover were these words, written in the Lakota language, one of many American Indian languages:

Woksape na Wounspe Wicohan Etan Woihanble Bluha Kte Lo

To find out what this message says, write the English translation
on the following blanks, using the Secret Code below. Then color the picture.

$\overline{13\ 25}$ $\overline{4\ 18\ 5\ 1\ 13\ 19}$ $\overline{23\ 9\ 12\ 12}$ $\overline{2\ 5\ 3\ 15\ 13\ 5}$ $\overline{18\ 5\ 1\ 12\ 9\ 20\ 25}$

$\overline{6\ 18\ 15\ 13}$ $\overline{2\ 5\ 3\ 15\ 13\ 9\ 14\ 7}$ $\overline{5\ 4\ 21\ 3\ 1\ 20\ 5\ 4}$ $\overline{1\ 14\ 4}$ $\overline{23\ 9\ 19\ 5}$

SECRET CODE

A	B	C	D	E	F	G	H	I	J	K	L	M	N	O	P	Q	R	S	T	U	V	W	X	Y	Z
1	2	3	4	5	6	7	8	9	10	11	12	13	14	15	16	17	18	19	20	21	22	23	24	25	26

Winter Count

As the Youngs left Pine Ridge, Mrs. Young told the children about her own graduation from college. When she was finished, Sarah said, "Hey, Mom, that's a neat story. I love to hear family stories over and over."

Mrs. Young said, "So do I. Telling family and tribal stories has always been very important for all American Indians. Traditions, customs, and history used to be passed down by word of mouth or by pictures, because there was no written language. Here, why don't you two children look at these pictures of some Lakota winter counts."

Mrs. Young explained that a tribe's winter count was like a calendar or diary drawn on an animal skin by the tribal historian. Each winter the tribal council chose the most important event of the year, and the historian recorded it on the hide with a simple drawing. He used the hide to keep track of time and to teach history. The famous Big Missouri Winter Count was kept from 1796 to 1926, and included records of the deaths of chiefs, peace treaties, a solar eclipse, and even a bank robbery! Look at the 1873 drawing representing Standing Cloud's new buffalo robe.

Mr. Young suggested that the children make winter counts of their own lives. This is what Andrew drew:

See if you can figure out Andrew's winter count and fill in the blanks. It has a drawing for each year of his life, starting at age 1 and running to age 11, when he took his trip across the country.

Andrew was only _____ when the Youngs vacationed in Hawaii. He learned to read when he was _____. Kitty became part of the family when Andrew was _____. Andrew got his first bike when he was _____. _____ years later, Andrew fell and broke his arm. When he was _____, he was in an earthquake. Andrew and Sarah got the chickenpox when he was _____. He was on a soccer team the year he turned _____. How old was Andrew when he moved to a new house? _____

Start your own winter count. Draw it on a big sheet of paper. The pictures can read across, like words on a page, or spiral out from the middle. Once you get up to this year, save the paper. Add a new picture each winter, perhaps on New Year's Day. Remember what each drawing is so you can tell your story to your grandchildren some day!

Bison, Bison

"Look!" exclaimed Sarah. "Buffalo!"

"There sure are," replied Mr. Young. "Just think, there used to be millions of buffalo living in great herds that stretched as far as you could see."

"Wow!" exclaimed Sarah as she gazed for miles over the flat, treeless plains.

"Buffalo used to be one of the main resources of the Plains Indians," continued Mr. Young. "They used every part of these huge creatures—from hide to hoof—for food, tools, clothing, and shelter."

Mrs. Young added. "You know, people call them buffalo, but their real name is bison."

She gave the children this puzzle and a list of a few of the more than 100 ways the Plains peoples used the buffalo. See if you can fit the items under "Uses" into the puzzle spaces. After you have filled in all the words, use the special symbol in each word to discover what part of the buffalo was used to make the object. For example, list any word with a ◯ in it under "Bones."

Uses

sled runners	cradle
winter robes	spoons
fresh meat	jerky (dried
tipi cover	meat)
game dice	knife
fly brush	shirt
leggings	whips
dresses	club
rattles	cups
scraper	fuel
shovels	glue

Used Parts

◯ Bones
_____
_____
_____
_____
_____
_____

☺ Horns
_____
_____

☐ Hide
_____
_____
_____
_____
_____

❄ Tail
_____
_____

❀ Hoof
_____

☼ Meat
_____
_____

☠ Buffalo Chips
(droppings, feces)
_____

American Indians Past and Present

"It sure was fun to see Aunt Lucy get her diploma! Maybe she'll become famous," Andrew mused. "Are there many famous American Indians, Dad?"

"Well, there have always been important American Indians," Mr. Young answered. "But for several reasons we often don't know much about them. I can tell you about a few famous folks."

Read about the Indians whom Mr. Young described; then play the game on pages 14-15.

Massasoit (17th Century)

Massasoit was the leader of the Wampanoags, the tribe that the Pilgrims met when they landed at Plymouth Rock in 1607. He signed the first treaty with the Pilgrims. Massasoit pledged not to hurt the Pilgrims or to steal from them, and then the Pilgrims agreed to help protect the Wampanoags from other Indian groups. Both groups kept their pledge.

The Wampanoags shared their food with the Pilgrims. Some people believe the two groups had a feast to celebrate the Pilgrims' first harvest.

Sacajawea (1787?-1812?)

In 1804 to 1806 the Lewis and Clark expedition traveled from the Missouri River to the Pacific Ocean. Few white men had seen this area.

Sacajawea, a Shoshone, helped to guide the explorers. She taught them which plants and animals to eat. Because she took her baby son, other Indians knew the explorers came in peace. No woman with a baby would lead a war party.

Many places, including a river, lake, and mountain pass, are named for Sacajawea. In fact, she has more memorials than any other American woman.

Geronimo (1829-1909)

Geronimo's Apache name was Goyanthlay, which means "One Who Yawns." The name suited him because he was easygoing, and for years he lived in peace.

Unfortunately, things changed when Mexican troops killed his family. He saw how first the Mexicans and then the European settlers took advantage of his people. He became a great warrior, holding his troops together with his leadership.

Geronimo was imprisoned several times by the U.S. government, but in 1905 he rode in Theodore Roosevelt's inaugural parade in Washington, D.C.

Jim Thorpe (1888-1953)

Jim Thorpe was descended from Black Hawk, a Sauk and Fox chief. Thorpe became one of the world's greatest athletes, starring in football, baseball, and track. In the 1912 Olympics he won several track events. Then for eight years he played baseball with the New York Giants and helped them win the World Series. Finally, until he was forty, he played pro football.

A town in Pennsylvania is named after him.

Maria Martinez (1887?-1980)

Maria Martinez is well known for her perfectly shaped pots. Her beautiful pottery was similar to very old pots of her people, the Pueblos. Although her pottery won many awards, she felt that her entire village should receive recognition. She, therefore, passed on her skills and knowledge to her relatives and others. Today her "black-on-black" pots sell for over $1,000.

Many museums exhibit her pottery, and once she was honored at the White House.

Ben Nighthorse Campbell (1933-)

Ben Nighthorse Campbell, a Cheyenne Indian, had a troubled childhood. He later learned discipline by studying judo, and became captain of the U.S. team in the 1964 Olympics. Finally, he got into politics, and in 1992 was elected senator from Colorado in the U.S. Senate.

He helped to create the American Indian College Fund, which helps young American Indians go to college. He also makes fine Native American jewelry that is often displayed in museums.

Wheel of History

After the Young children had heard the stories of the six famous American Indians, they wanted to play "Wheel of History." You can play it, too, but **STOP!** You need to read "American Indians Past and Present" on page 13 or you won't do well.

HOW TO PLAY

Two to four people can play. Each person needs a button or other small marker, and you need two coins to share. Each player also needs a pencil and a piece of paper to keep score. Each one of you should make a chart by (1) writing the name of each famous person on page 13 down the left side of the paper and (2) writing your own name at the top. To win, you must have the most correct answers on your sheet at the end of the game.

1. Place all markers at "START HERE." The youngest player goes first.

2. To move, toss both coins. The number of heads you get (none, one, or two) is the number of spaces you may move forward. You may move along any path and go in either direction around the circle, and two markers may share the same space. **A turn consists of only one throw.**

3. You can land on three types of spaces:

♦ **"You did it!" squares.** Follow the directions.

♦ **Question squares.** Read the question out loud and decide which famous person it matches. Write the number of the question in your column next to that famous person's name, and then move your marker to that famous person's circle. If at any time during the game you land on another question that you think matches a person you have already guessed, you may also write that number down next to the correct person. If you land on a question a second time, you do not answer it and your turn ends.

♦ **Famous person circles.** If you land on a circle when you throw the coins, put a star in your column next to that famous person's name.

4. The game is over when a player has written a number or a star next to each famous person and, thus, "goes out." For a longer game, play until someone has a star next to each famous person's name.

5. To see who won, check each player's answers against the list on the back cover. Award 10 points for each correct answer, 5 points for each star, and 5 points to the player who goes out first. The player with the highest score wins.

Map Fun. These six famous American Indians were from different tribes. On the map on pages 2-3 find the state where many people from each tribe live and write the tribe's name in it: **Apache** (Arizona), **Cheyenne** (Oklahoma), **Pueblo** (New Mexico), **Sauk and Fox** (Iowa), **Shoshone** (Nevada), and **Wampanoag** (Massachusetts).

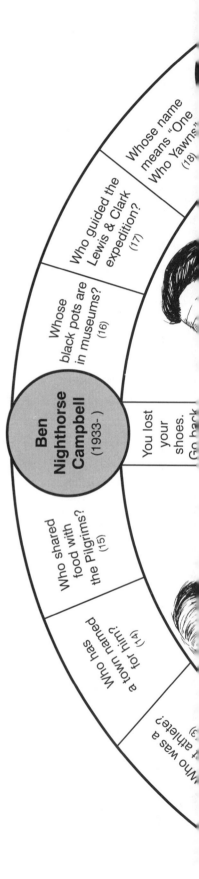

Whose name means "One Who Yawns" (18)

Who guided the Lewis & Clark expedition? (17)

Whose black pots are in museums? (16)

Ben Nighthorse Campbell (1933-)

You lost your shoes. Go back.

Who shared food with the Pilgrims? (15)

Who has a town named for him? (14)

Who was a athlete? (13)

Who was a strong Apache leader? (1)

Who makes beautiful Native American jewelry? (2)

Who was elected to the U.S. Senate? (3)

Massasoit (17th Century)

Sacajawea (1787?-1812?)

You took a nap. Lose a turn.

You got bored. Go back 1 space.

Who signed a treaty with the Pilgrims? (4)

Who won Olympic medals in track? (5)

You're eager to win. Go ahead 1 space.

You took a vitamin pill. Go ahead 4 spaces.

Who was honored at the White House? (6)

START HERE

You love history. Go ahead 1 space.

You're talking on the phone. Lose a turn.

Geronimo (1829-1909)

You have high hopes. Go ahead 1 space.

You ate your Wheaties. Go ahead 4 spaces.

You ate your spinach. Go ahead 1 space.

You stumbled and fell. Go back 1 spaces.

Who knew all about wild foods? (7)

Who was leader of the Wampanoags? (8)

You forgot to study. Go back 1 space.

Who was good at judo? (11)

Who has many places named for her? (12)

Who fought for his people's rights? (10)

Who became a well-known potter? (9)

Maria Martinez (1887?-1980)

Jim Thorpe (1888-1953)

Powwow!

"I can't believe we're almost in Wisconsin!" Sarah sighed after a long afternoon in the car."

"*I* can't believe I get to dance in the powwow tomorrow!" chimed in Andrew. "Mom, are you sure it'll be like the powwows at home?"

"Yes," answered Mrs. Young. "This one is sponsored by the Ojibwa in Wisconsin, Andrew, but all powwows across the United States are pretty much the same. You'll find

American Indian people of all ages and tribes dancing, singing, and visiting with friends and relatives—just like our powwows at home."

Mr. Young broke in, "But what's most important is that they're special times when we Indians can think about who we are and can celebrate and preserve the old ways of our ancestors."

Andrew closed his eyes and smiled as he thought about how he would dance at the powwow tomorrow.

POWWOW DANCERS

Each powwow has a person to announce the different events, one or more groups of drummers to sing and beat rhythms on a large drum, and, of course, lots of dancers. The main kinds of dances are traditional dances, fancy (including shawl) dances, grass dances, and jingle dances. You can tell the dancers apart by their outfits and by the kinds of dancing they do. Each powwow begins with the grand entry, when all the dancers line up and enter the powwow circle to dance together.

Look at the six descriptions of powwow dancers on this page. Match each with the correct drawing on page 17 by putting the letter of the description on the line by the correct picture.

A. Male traditional dancer. His outfit represents clothing worn in the early 1800s. He wears some combination of a deerskin breechcloth, feathered headpiece, moccasins, leggings, and a bustle. (A bustle is a circle of feathers worn on the back.)

B. Female traditional dancer. She wears a cloth or hide outfit with beadwork and carries a beautiful shawl over one arm.

C. Male fancy dancer. His outfit is based on traditional clothing but practically explodes with bright colors, shiny sequins, and ribbons. He wears two bustles.

D. Female fancy shawl dancer. This young woman wears a fancy shawl over her shoulders and holds the ends in her hands as she dances.

E. Male grass dancer. He wears long yarn or ribbon fringe that hangs from his shoulders, waist, and legs. He carries a feather fan and does not wear a bustle.

F. Female jingle dancer. Her outfit is covered with rows of thin metal cones that jingle when she dances.

Don't forget that page 28 has pronunciations of difficult words. It also tells you about some good books on American Indians.

1. _____

2. _____

3. _____

4. _____

5. _____

6. _____

USE THESE CLUES!

Now, if you are ready for a challenge, check out your detective skills. Here are clues describing the dance steps of five of the dancers. Write the number of the correct drawing on the following lines. (The last clue has two answers.)

_____ a. This male dancer stoops and makes dramatic movements, imitating animals, birds, or a hunter tracking them.

_____ b. This dancer makes graceful bends and gentle hops, creating jingling sounds to match the rhythm of the drumbeats.

_____ c. This male dancer moves like long, waving prairie grasses.

_____ _____ d. These fancily dressed dancers make quick steps and fast turns in energetic dances requiring great endurance.

Be sure to check your answers on the back cover.

Psst. You can imagine that *you* are in a powwow. Try the steps described to the right.

17

The Good Berry

Mrs. Young had bought a book on the Ojibwa people, and as they left Wisconsin, she suggested that the children read it aloud as they traveled.

Sarah began, "The area around the Great Lakes is beautiful . . ."

"You bet it is," chimed in Andrew.

"Stop interrupting," snapped Sarah, who began again. "The area around the Great Lakes is beautiful but has short, dry summers and long, cold winters. The Ojibwa and other Native people in this area traveled with the changing seasons to those areas providing the best food and protection."

"Just like the Suquamish," interrupted Andrew.

"Mother, make him stop!" cried Sarah. Then she continued: "In early fall the Ojibwa hunted game for meat and hides. In winter they moved to the woods in small groups, sharing food and making and repairing tools, baskets, and clothes. When March came, the Ojibwa headed for maple tree groves to collect sap for maple sugar. They re-

turned to their villages in summer to fish, gather wild nuts and berries, and tend gardens.

"In September, the Ojibwa went to shallow lakes and streams to harvest a wild marsh plant they called *manomin,* or the 'good berry.' They collected the ripe *manomin* by canoe. A man would paddle while a woman bent the stalks over the canoe and hit them with a short paddle until the *manomin* dropped into the canoe. They always left some *manomin* on the stalks to fall into the water and grow into new plants next year. On shore, the *manomin* was dried, roasted, and stored in twine bags. This food kept the Ojibwa going through the long, hard winter."

You may know *manomin* by another name. See if you can figure it out by following the directions below as you travel around the marsh. Every time you stop, collect a letter. (Only collect a letter when you stop.) Write the letters in the exact order that you collect them to complete this sentence:

Manomin is also called _ _ _ _   _ _ _ _ _ .

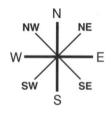

1. Start at canoe. Paddle south 3 squares.

2. Leave canoe and walk southeast 2 squares into woods.

3. Go north 4 squares, crossing stream on stepping stones.

4. Walk east 3 squares and pick up extra bags.

5. Go south 4 squares to explore edge of new marsh.

6. Move northwest 1 square.

7. Travel north 4 squares through berry thickets.

8. Go west 3 squares to return to lake.

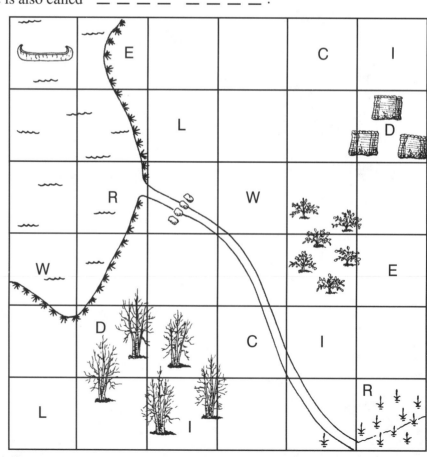

What's in a Name?

Andrew was very quiet as they rode along. Finally, he said, "Dad, we're Cherokee *and* American Indian *and* Washingtonian *and* American, right?"

Mr. Young answered, "Yes, Andrew, that's certainly all true."

A little puzzled, Andrew continued, "Well, does everyone have so many names?"

His dad said, "Sure. Sometimes people use different names for the same things."

"Like what, Dad?" piped up Sarah.

Mrs. Young said, "You can find the answer by solving this puzzle.

Put the first letter and every third letter after that in the blanks by Janice's picture. (Psst. It will help to cross out each letter as you use it.) Then put the second letter and every third letter after that in the blanks by Bill's picture. The remaining letters go with Nora's picture.

A N F M A I E T R R I S I V T C E N A A A N M T I E I N R O D I N I C S A A ! N N

I'm an
_ _ _ _ _ _ _
_ _ _ _ _ .

Please call me
_ _ _ _ _ _
_ _ _ _ _ _ _ _ .

Bill

Janice

Nora

In Canada, we are called
_ _ _ _ _
_ _ _ _ _ _ _ !

When the children finished, Andrew understood and added, "Oh yeah! And some people use their tribal name, like Suquamish or Lakota, right?"

"You've got it, Andrew," replied Mrs. Young.

How many words can you think of to identify *you?* To get you started, consider where you live, who your ancestors were (like African, European, Hispanic, Asian, and so on), and any groups you belong to.

The People of the Longhouse

The Youngs were going to visit Lisa next. The children had met Lisa at the Wisconsin powwow, and Lisa's mom had invited them for dinner. Lisa lives on the Onondaga reservation in New York State.

The Onondaga are one of the six Iroquois nations. Back in the early 1500s, five similar American Indian groups banded together into a family of tribes called the Iroquois Confederacy. (The sixth group, the Tuscarora, joined in the 1720s.) The kind of government they set up has lasted until today. It even influenced Benjamin Franklin in his ideas of forming the U.S. government.

The Iroquois and other American Indians of the Northeast lived in rich forests. They had plenty of trees for shelter and fuel, many lakes and rivers for fresh water, and lots of game and fish for meat. They hunted, but they also farmed crops (especially corn, beans, and squash) and gathered wild plants. Because resources were so plentiful, the Iroquois settled in villages that had from one hundred to thousands of people. They lived in large bark and log longhouses that held several families.

The original five nations of the Iroquois Confederacy called themselves the "People of the Longhouse." Today each has a reservation in New York State. Find the five dots showing the locations of the reservations on the map on page 21. Figure out which nation lives on which reservation by using the clues next to the map. Write each nation's letter on the correct line.

After the children had finished the map activity, Andrew commented, "I can't wait to see Lisa. I think it's cool she's Wolf."

"What do you mean?" asked Sarah, puzzled.

"Wolf is her clan," explained Mrs. Young. "A clan is a group of related people within a tribe who can trace their family back to a common ancestor. Iroquois clans name themselves after special animals.

"A long time ago clans became scattered among many villages. No matter where you traveled, though, you'd be welcome in the longhouse of people who were of the same clan as you."

Mr. Young added, "You know how you children have my last name? Well, Iroquois clans are handed down through the mothers. Lisa is part of the Wolf clan—the same clan as her mother and her grandmother and her great-grandmother. Not all Native Americans have clans, but the Onondaga have nine, each named after an animal." And he named the clans.

Sarah announced, "I'd like to be Bear—he's the biggest and toughest of them all."

CLUES

A. Mohawks, Keepers of the Eastern Door

B. Onondagas, Keepers of the Central Fire

C. Senecas, Keepers of the Western Door

D. Oneidas, Little Brother of the Eastern Door Keepers

E. Cayugas, Little Brother of the Western Door Keepers

Psst. Don't forget to put these New York tribes on the big map on pages 2-3.

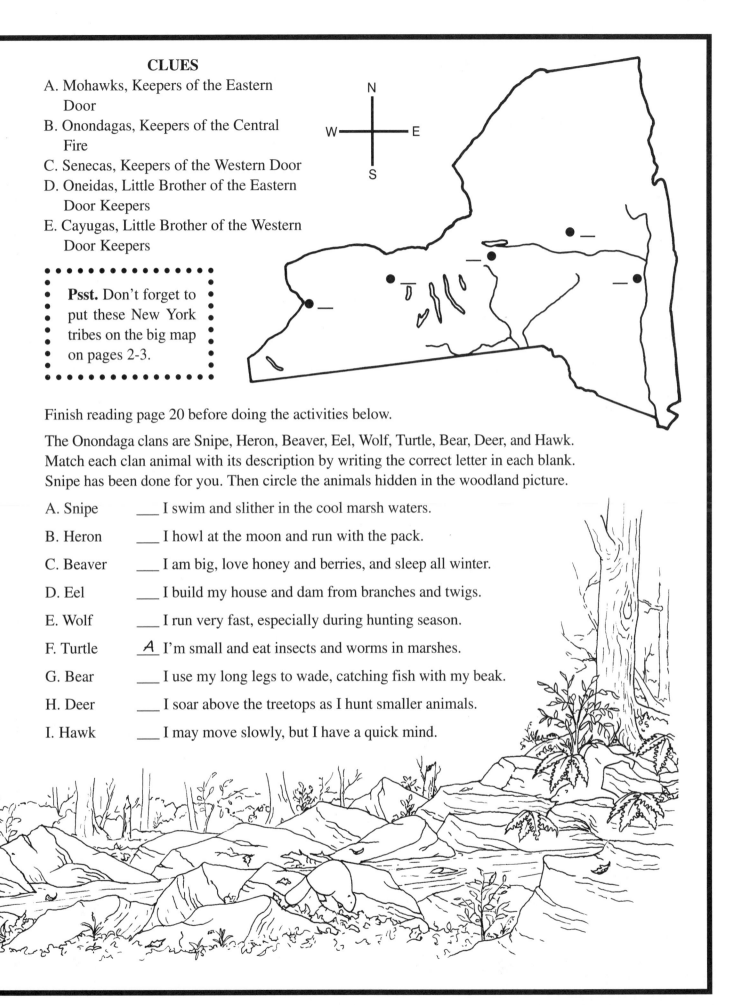

Finish reading page 20 before doing the activities below.

The Onondaga clans are Snipe, Heron, Beaver, Eel, Wolf, Turtle, Bear, Deer, and Hawk. Match each clan animal with its description by writing the correct letter in each blank. Snipe has been done for you. Then circle the animals hidden in the woodland picture.

A. Snipe   ___ I swim and slither in the cool marsh waters.

B. Heron   ___ I howl at the moon and run with the pack.

C. Beaver   ___ I am big, love honey and berries, and sleep all winter.

D. Eel   ___ I build my house and dam from branches and twigs.

E. Wolf   ___ I run very fast, especially during hunting season.

F. Turtle   *A* I'm small and eat insects and worms in marshes.

G. Bear   ___ I use my long legs to wade, catching fish with my beak.

H. Deer   ___ I soar above the treetops as I hunt smaller animals.

I. Hawk   ___ I may move slowly, but I have a quick mind.

Knock, Knock, Who's in There?

Lisa, Andrew, and Sarah worked this puzzle. See if you can solve it too. Here's what you do. First, do the math problems; then find each answer in the mystery picture. (You'll find each answer more than once.) Color the picture as follows:

• Brown for addition answers   • Green for multiplication answers
• Orange for division answers   • Yellow for subtraction answers

When the picture is finished, solve the three riddles below.

98 − 8 = _____	27 ÷ 3 = _____
9 + 4 = _____	62 + 110 = _____
12 × 3 = _____	600 − 584 = _____
17 + 6 = _____	66 + 11 = _____
10 ÷ 5 = _____	5 × 14 = _____
102 + 44 = _____	5 + 14 = _____
100 − 66 = _____	420 ÷ 4 = _____
39 + 12 = _____	32 + 32 = _____
16 × 5 = _____	90 − 60 = _____
500 + 69 = _____	90 + 60 = _____
144 ÷ 12 = _____	600 − 575 = _____
144 + 144 = _____	15 × 15 = _____

KNOCK, KNOCK, WHO'S IN THERE?

Guess which tribal nation. Oneida (New York), Navajo (Arizona), or Crow (Montana)

Guess which houses. tipis, hogans, or longhouses

1. We used to live in houses made from animal skins sewn together. We could move our houses when hunting got difficult.

We are _____ , and our ancestors lived in

_____ .

2. Some of us still live in these houses built of dirt and wood with dome-shaped roofs. We live near the Hopi nation.

We are _____ , and some of us still live in

_____ .

3. Our ancestors lived with several other families in long, rectangular houses made of wood. Their villages were near forests.

We are _____ , and once we lived in

_____ .

•••••••••••••••••••••
• Put the tribes' names on •
• the map on pages 2-3. •
•••••••••••••••••••••

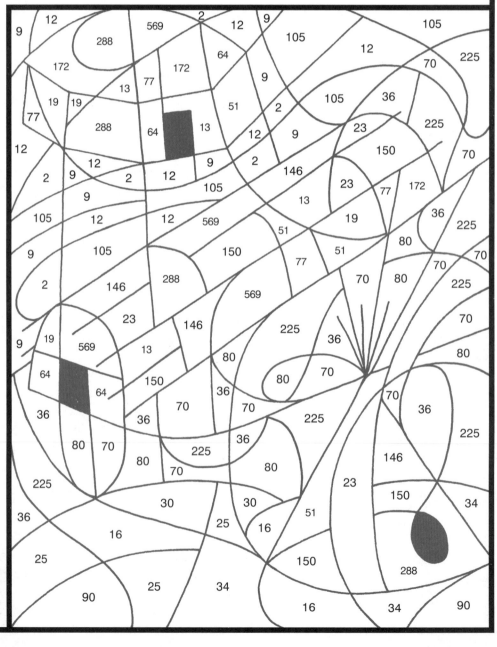

Feasting and Friendship

Andrew and Sarah had a lot of fun with their friend Lisa, but it was time to head for Massachusetts. A Wampanoag friend of Mr. Young's had invited them to a clambake there. Both children wanted to know what it would be like, and Andrew asked his dad to tell him a little about the Wampanoag nation.

Mr. Young explained, "The Wampanoags were the first people the Pilgrims met in the New World. Led by Chief Massasoit, the Wampanoags shared their food with the Pilgrims and helped them survive their first hard winter. Massasoit also made a peace treaty with the English that lasted for more than fifty years. Although not everyone agrees, some folks believe the Indians and the Pilgrims showed their friendship by sharing a great feast to celebrate the Pilgrim's first harvest."

Mrs. Young spoke up, "Feasts are still important events for the Wampanoags. In fact, a clambake, or *appanaug*, is one type of feast. More than just a meal or picnic, the *appanaug* is a special celebration. Sometimes it honors an important person, but it's always a chance to share tribal traditions.

"The traditional way of cooking is to prepare a bed of rocks in a fire. The hot rocks are covered with seaweed to protect the food from scorching. Then corn, potatoes, onions, clams, lobsters, and other foods are put on the rocks to cook. After several hours, the food is ready."

"Yum!" said Sarah. "I can't wait!"

Mr. Young told everyone a funny story about a boy who loved *appanaugs*. The Wampanoags harvested and gathered so many good foods from the land and caught so many delicious kinds of seafood that it was hard for him to decide which kind of food was the best! To discover his favorite dish, look at these pictures and follow the directions.

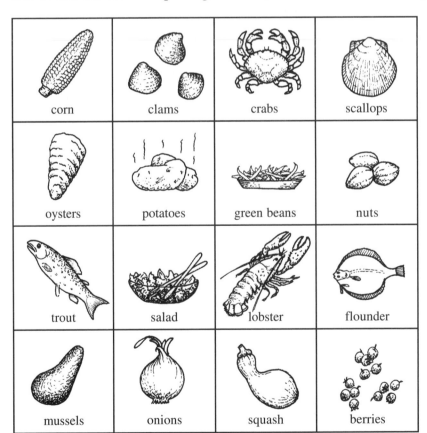

1. Put your finger on any of the seafood dishes you see here.

2. Now move your finger LEFT or RIGHT to the nearest food grown on land.

3. Then move your finger UP or DOWN to the nearest seafood.

4. Now move in a DIAGONAL direction to the nearest food grown on land.

5. Then move DOWN or RIGHT to the nearest seafood.

Now you know the boy's favorite food! Do the puzzle again, starting on another seafood— the answer is always the same!

 Psst. If you want to know how to pronounce *appanaug,* turn to page 28.

Page 28 also lists some books you may enjoy reading.

23

Region of Plenty

After the clambake, the Youngs left for their final destination—Grandma's. But before they reached her house, they stopped at the Cherokee reservation in North Carolina. At the museum there, Andrew and Sarah learned about the life of the Cherokees and other tribal nations that have lived in the Southeast of what is now the United States.

Because of the mild climate and good soil, these American Indians grew a variety of foods. The area's rich forests, rivers, and marshes offered plentiful natural resources too. With such a steady supply of fresh water and food from the environment, these groups could stay in one place all year round. Several large southeastern tribes such as the Creeks and Cherokees formed permanent villages and towns with good-sized populations.

Five of the largest tribal nations in the Southeast—the Cherokees, Choctaws, Seminoles, Creeks, and Chickasaws—were known by the Europeans as the Five Civilized Tribes. Use the clues below to figure out where the tribes lived.

Read the four sentences under the map. Decide where each tribal nation was located and write its name on the correct line on the map. (Hint: Read all of the statements first.)

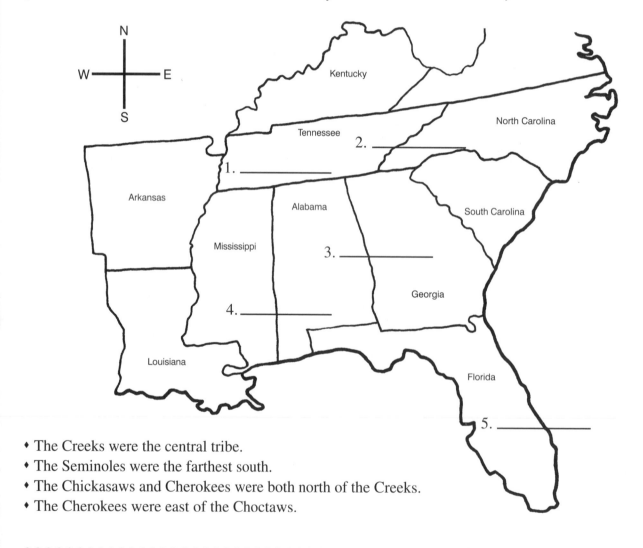

- The Creeks were the central tribe.
- The Seminoles were the farthest south.
- The Chickasaws and Cherokees were both north of the Creeks.
- The Cherokees were east of the Choctaws.

Don't forget to put these nations' names on the map on pages 2-3.

The Cherokee Alphabet

While the Youngs were at the museum, Andrew discovered an exhibit on Sequoyah, a famous Cherokee. Sequoyah lived from about 1760 to 1843. Although he never learned to read or write the English language, he was very interested in the way Europeans used "talking leaves" (writing) to share ideas. He spent more than ten years creating a Cherokee alphabet, or *syllabary*.

Sequoyah

The Cherokee still use this syllabary today. It has eighty-six symbols, only a few of which are shown here. Some of the symbols will look familiar to you, because Sequoyah based many of his characters on our Latin alphabet. However, there is no relationship between Cherokee characters and letters in the English alphabet. For example, the Cherokee "**Z**" is pronounced "no," and the character "**M**" is pronounced "lu."

It was easier for the Cherokee to learn to write their language than it was to learn English. In a short time many Cherokee could read and write. They had already developed their own towns, laws, and a democratic form of government. Now they could read. They even published their own newspaper. They were truly creative people of the nineteenth century.

However, many white settlers still considered the Cherokee barbarians. The settlers wanted more and more property and tried to force the Indians to leave their homeland. In 1838 the U.S. government ordered the Cherokee people to leave their towns and farms, and to head west to the newly created Indian Territory. They had to march hundreds of miles during a harsh winter. The men, women, and children took only what they could

carry on their backs. More than 4,000 of the 17,000 American Indians died along the way. This tragic journey is called the "Trail of Tears."

Some Cherokee stayed behind and their descendants live in North Carolina. Many Cherokee today, though, live in the state created from the former Indian Territory. To figure out the name of this state, write the sound of each of the following Cherokee characters on the line below it.

ꙮ Ꙫ W ꜰ ꙅ

—— —— —— —— ——

Then sound out all the syllables. The old Indian Territory is now the state of

—— —— —— —— —— —— ——.

D	R	T	ꙮ	Ꙫ
a	e	i	o	u
S	Ꮞ	Ꮀ	Ꮁ	Ꮝ
ga	ge	ha	ho	ka
W	Ꮙ	M	ꙅ	Ꮧ
la	le	lu	ma	me
Λ	Z	Ꮒ	Ꮰ	Ꮞ
ne	no	sa	so	su
W	Ꮏ	Ꮽ	Ꮣ	Ꮗ
ta	te	we	ya	yo

Try writing some of the Cherokee letters on the following lines. Imagine how Sequoyah's people felt when they learned to read and write!

A *syllabary* is a list of sounds (or syllables) that make up a written language. (Syllabary, syllables—get the connection?)

———————————————

———————————————

Grandma's House

Finally, the Youngs reached the end of their long journey—Grandma's home in Bryson City, North Carolina. They hurried from the car to her apartment, where Grandma met them with hugs, smiles, and a just-delivered pizza. "Sorry about the dinner," she apologized, "but I had to work late at the library. We'll make up for it tomorrow with a home-cooked Cherokee feast!"

Both children helped in the kitchen the next day. As they cut vegetables for Grandma's beef stew with dumplings, she explained that as a child, she often ate squirrel or rabbit meat. Grandma told them the legend of Kana'ti, the first man on earth, and the origin of game hunting. "In the time soon after the world was created, no hunting was necessary. However, Kana'ti's rascal sons let all the wild deer escape from their special place under a large rock, and from that time on Indians had to work hard to hunt wild animals for food. . . . I re-member the good taste of my mother's rabbit stew, but I'm glad I can buy beef at the grocery store nowadays!" laughed Grandma.

They fixed green beans and sweet potatoes baked with nuts. Then they made creamy corn pudding and corn on the cob.

After Sarah mentioned how important corn was in traditional Hopi weddings, Grandma told them about the Cherokee Green Corn Ceremony. This feast celebrates the end of summer when the first corn crop has ripened and the people look to a good harvest.

"I think everything's ready now," Grandma said, "so let's sit down to our own little feast."

After dinner, everyone spent the evening looking through Grandma's photo albums and scrapbooks. Sarah especially liked the pictures of Grandma as a girl on the reservation in North Carolina and her old report cards. Many pages of the scrapbooks were filled with clippings from Cherokee newspapers, including many articles about local news and editorials on national events. Grandma had an interesting story to go with each item in the books.

"Gee," Andrew said as the children finally went to bed, "I've learned more about our family and tribe tonight than I ever thought I would! Thanks, Grandma, for sharing all your memories with us."

Grandma replied, "I think it's important for you to know your background and traditions. I try to keep all these books labeled, but so much more is carried here," and she pointed to her head and heart. "May you always keep it so."

For a special treat the next morning, Grandma and the children made corn cakes, a traditional Cherokee food. You can try this recipe too. Be sure to have an adult help you, especially when frying the cakes.

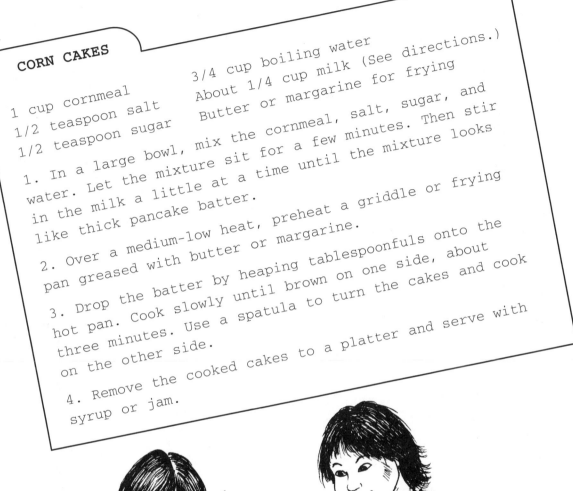

CORN CAKES

1 cup cornmeal
1/2 teaspoon salt
1/2 teaspoon sugar

3/4 cup boiling water
About 1/4 cup milk (See directions.)
Butter or margarine for frying

1. In a large bowl, mix the cornmeal, salt, sugar, and water. Let the mixture sit for a few minutes. Then stir in the milk a little at a time until the mixture looks like thick pancake batter.

2. Over a medium-low heat, preheat a griddle or frying pan greased with butter or margarine.

3. Drop the batter by heaping tablespoonfuls onto the hot pan. Cook slowly until brown on one side, about three minutes. Use a spatula to turn the cakes and cook on the other side.

4. Remove the cooked cakes to a platter and serve with syrup or jam.

During breakfast, everpyone raved over the corn cakes, and the children felt very proud.

"I'm so glad, Grandma," Andrew exclaimed, "that Sarah and I will be spending the rest of the summer with you."

"Me too!" chimed in Sarah. "I want to hear more stories you learned when you were a girl."

Neither Mr. or Mrs. Young reminded her not to speak with her mouth full. They just smiled. They both knew that their children were learning how to balance their lives as American Indians with their other lives in the city.

Pronunciations

Here are all the tribal nations mentioned in this book. Also note the lists of people, places, and other difficult words.

TRIBAL NATIONS
(Remember, there are about 500 tribes altogether.)
Apache, ah-PAT-chee
Calusa, kah-LOO-sah
Cayuga, kah-U-gah
Cherokee, CHAIR-oh-kee
Cheyenne, shy-YEN
Chickasaw, CHICK-ah-saw
Choctaw, CHALK-tah
Comanche, ko-MAN-chee
Creek, CREEK
Diné, deh-NAY
Fox, FOX
Hopi, HO-pee
Iowa, I-oh-wah
Iroquois, EAR-ah-koy
Lakota, lah-KO-tah
Miami, my-AM-ee
Miwok, MEE-walk

Mohawk, MO-hawk
Narragansett, NAH-rah-GAN-set
Navajo, NAH-vah-ho
Ojibwa, oh-JIB-way
Oglala, o-GLAH-lah
Oneida, o-NI-dah
Onondaga, AH-non-DAH-gah
Salish, SAY-lish
Sauk, SAWK
Seminole, SEM-in-ole
Seneca, SEN-eh-kah
Pueblo, PWEB-lo
Shoshone, sho-SHO-nee
Sioux, SUE
Suquamish, sue-QUAM-ish
Susquehannock, SUH-sque-
   HAN-nock
Tuscarora, TUS-kah-ROAR-ah
Wampanoag, WAHM-pah-no-ahg
Yakima, YAH-kah-mah

PEOPLE
Geronimo, jeh-RON-i-mo
Martinez, mar-TIN-ez
Massasoit, MASS-sah-soit

Sacajawea, SAH-kah-jah-WE-ah
Sequoyah, seh-KOY-yah
Sealth, CELL-thah
Talayesva, TAH-lah-YES-vah

PLACES
Kittanning, kit-TAN-ning
Kittatinny, KIT-tah-TIN-ee
Loyalhanna, LOY-ahl-HAN-nah
Manhattan, man-HAT-tan
Moenkopi, mo-in-KO-pee
Seattle, sea-AT-tall
Susquehanna, SUS-que-HAN-nah
Tunkhannock, TUNK-han-nock

MISCELLANEOUS
appanaug, AH-pan-ahg
Hispanic, hiss-PAN-ic
Kana'ti, kah-NAH-tee
manomin, MAH-no-min
mesa, MAY-sah
piki, PEE-kee
reservation, REH-ser-VA-shon
syllabary, SIL-lah-BEAR-ee

Good Books to Read

You can learn more about your American Indian neighbors by reading these books.

Hoyt-Goldsmith, Diane. *Cherokee Summer.* New York: Holiday House, 1993.
Ten-year-old Bridget shares her personal history and that of her tribe.

Monture, Joel. *Cloudwalker: Contemporary Native American Stories.* Colorado: Fulcrum Publishing, 1996.
These stories deal with the way Native children straddle two cultures in both a funny and a sad way.

Peters, Russel M. *Clambake: A Wampanoag Tradition.* Minneapolis: Lerner Publications, 1992.
Steven, a Wampanoag, tells you more about the *appanaug* ceremony.

Ortiz, Simon. *The People Shall Continue.* San Francisco: Children's Book Press, 1988.
This epic story of Native people speaks in rhythms of oral narrative.

Regguinti, Gordon. *The Sacred Harvest: Ojibway Wild Rice Gathering.* Minneapolis: Lerner Publications, 1992.
Learn more about harvesting wild rice as you travel with the Ojibway.

Stein, R. Conrad. *The Trail of Tears.* Danbury, CT: Children's Press, 1993.
This book depicts the long journey the Cherokees and others were forced to take as they were relocated.

Sweatzell, Rina. *Children of Clay: A Family of Pueblo Potters.* Minneapolis: Lerner Publications, 1992.
Learn how Pueblo Indians of the Southwest pass their tradition of pottery-making from generation to generation.

FOR ADULTS
Slapin, Beverly. *How to Tell the Difference: A Checklist for Evaluating Children's Books for Anti-Indian Bias.* Berkeley, CA: Oyate Press, 1995.